Copyright © 2024 Gloria Greene

All rights reserved. No portion of this book may be reproduced in any form without permission from the publisher, except as permitted by U.S. copyright law.

For permissions contact info@gloriagreene.com

How To Use Positive Affirmations

CHOOSE AFFIRMATIONS

Flip through the pages of this book and select affirmations that align with your goals, desires, and values. Whether you're focusing on career, self-love, finances, family, or overall well-being, choose phrases that feel meaningful and inspire you.

Tip: If a particular affirmation doesn't feel right at first, it's okay! Sometimes, our subconscious resists new ideas. Stick with it—it's part of the process.

CREATE A VISION BOARD

Cut out your chosen affirmations and pair them with images that reflect your dreams. Arrange them on a vision board to create a visual and emotional representation of the life you want to manifest. Place your vision board somewhere you'll see daily, like your bedroom or workspace.

REPEAT DAILY

Repetition is key to reinforcing new neural pathways in your brain. Take a few moments each day to say your affirmations out loud or in your mind. Speak with conviction, as if the statement is already true.

Example: Instead of thinking, I want to be confident, declare, I am confident and capable in every situation.

USE AFFIRMATIONS WITH MEDITATION AND TAPPING

Pair your affirmations with mindfulness practices like meditation or tapping (Emotional Freedom Technique). These techniques calm your mind, reduce resistance, and enhance your focus, making it easier to internalize positive thoughts.

- Meditation: Sit quietly, close your eyes, and visualize your affirmations coming to life.

- Tapping: Gently tap specific points on your body while repeating your affirmations to release emotional blocks.

BE CONSISTENT AND PATIENT

Positive affirmations work through repetition and consistency. Over time, your brain will create new neural pathways, replacing old, negative feedback loops with positive, empowering ones. It may feel awkward at first, but with daily practice, it will become effortless.

BELIEVE IN THE PROCESS

Science shows that your thoughts shape your reality. By focusing on positive affirmations, you train your brain to see opportunities, attract positivity, and take inspired action. Trust that the process is working, even if you don't see immediate results.

By consistently using positive affirmations, you'll rewire your brain to focus on the good, break free from limiting beliefs, and unlock the mental strength to achieve anything you set your mind to.
Start today, and watch as your life transforms one thought at a time.

I choose joy

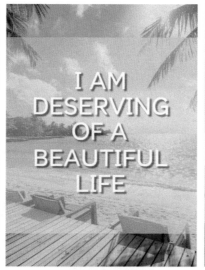

I AM DESERVING OF A BEAUTIFUL LIFE

I WILL TREAT MY BODY WITH THE RESPECT AND ACCEPTANCE IT DESERVES

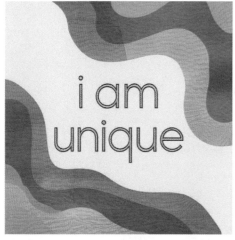

I am worthy of healing and recovery

I AM SMART

I AM CAPABLE AND CONFIDENT

i am unique

I deserve to be heard

I AM DESERVING OF LOVE

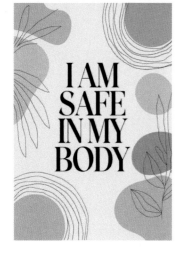

I AM SAFE IN MY BODY

MY VOICE AND NEEDS ARE IMPORTANT

I am Valued

I AM ENOUGH

I am capable of sitting with and allowing uncomfortable feelings

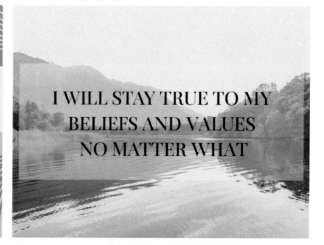

I WILL STAY TRUE TO MY BELIEFS AND VALUES NO MATTER WHAT

It's OK to ask for help and accept it gracefully

I am loved

I AM DESERVING OF REST, RELAXATION, AND RECOVERY

My needs are important

I DESERVE TO BE SEEN

I AM STRONG

I CAN TUNE INTO MY BODY TO DISCOVER WHAT IT NEEDS

A bad day does not not equal a bad life

I can choose which thoughts I believe and how I respond

I AM FIERCE

I was doing *the best I could* at the time with what I knew

I AM NOT DEFINED BY THE THOUGHTS THAT POP INTO MY HEAD

I will treat myself how I treat my best friend

MY MIND IS CALM AND MY BODY IS RELAXED

I AM BRAVE

I LOVE AND ACCEPT ALL PARTS OF MYSELF

I SEARCH FOR MOMENTS TO BE GRATEFUL FOR

I AM HONEST

MY WORTH IS NOT DETERMINED BY WHAT OTHERS THINK OF ME

THERE ARE NO LIMITS TO WHAT I CAN ACCOMPLISH

I am capable of growth and change

I am kind

I have the STRENGTH to make it through TOUGH TIMES

I WELCOME ABUNDANCE INTO MY LIFE

I DESERVE TO FEEL LIKE I BELONG, BECAUSE I DO.

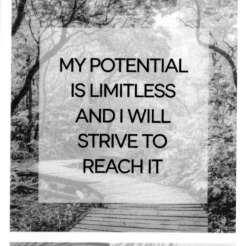
MY POTENTIAL IS LIMITLESS AND I WILL STRIVE TO REACH IT

I TRUST THE PATH THAT I AM ON

I AM SAFE IN THIS MOMENT

IT'S OK TO TAKE A BREAK

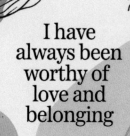
I have always been worthy of love and belonging

I HAVE EVERYTHING I NEED WITHIN ME TO HEAL

I AM FREE

I am

I am

I am

I am

I am

I am

I deserve

I deserve

I deserve

I deserve

I deserve

I deserve

IT IS OK TO PUT PUT MY NEEDS FIRST

I WILL STAY FOCUSSED ON MY DREAMS

I am perfect just the way I am

I see beauty in all of me, even the imperfections

I HAVE THE POWER TO MAKE TODAY A GREAT DAY

I AM UNIQUE AND AMAZING

I DO WHAT BRINGS ME JOY

i find JOY in the smallest of moments

I CHOOSE PROGRESS OVER PERFECTION

I am patient enough to wait for what I deserve

I am strong enough to let go

I AM HEALING MY BODY WITH EACH MOUTHFUL

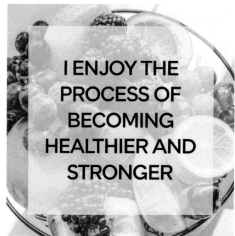
I ENJOY THE PROCESS OF BECOMING HEALTHIER AND STRONGER

MY HEALTH IS A PRIORITY FOR ME

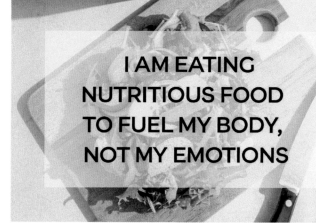
I AM EATING NUTRITIOUS FOOD TO FUEL MY BODY, NOT MY EMOTIONS

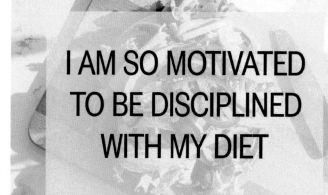
I AM SO MOTIVATED TO BE DISCIPLINED WITH MY DIET

I AM POWERFUL ENOUGH TO RESIST TEMPTATIONS

I HONOR MY BODY BY GIVING IT WHAT IT TRULY NEEDS

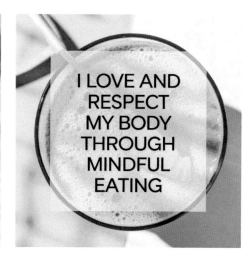
I LOVE AND RESPECT MY BODY THROUGH MINDFUL EATING

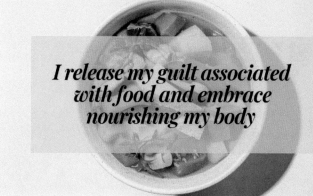
I release my guilt associated with food and embrace nourishing my body

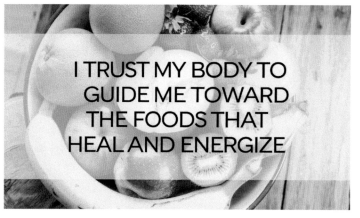
I TRUST MY BODY TO GUIDE ME TOWARD THE FOODS THAT HEAL AND ENERGIZE

EVERY WORKOUT BRINGS ME CLOSER TO MY FITNESS GOALS

I AM STRONG AND POWERFUL

EXERCISE IS A CELEBRATION OF WHAT MY BODY CAN DO

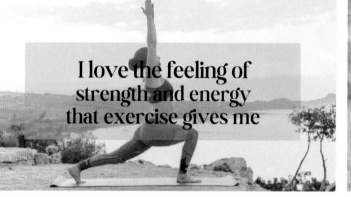

I love the feeling of strength and energy that exercise gives me

MY BODY IS BECOMING STRONGER AND MORE RESILIENT WITH EACH MOVEMENT

I am committed to making exercise a regular part of my healthy lifestyle

I CRUSH ALL MY FITNESS GOALS

I WORKOUT TO HONOR MY BODY, IT'S STRENGTH AND IT'S GRIT

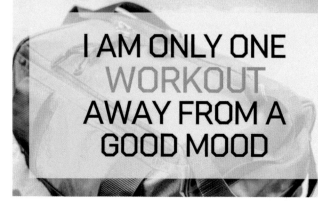

I AM ONLY ONE WORKOUT AWAY FROM A GOOD MOOD

MY BODY IS AMAZING

I am attracting the right person for me

I AM MAKING ROOM FOR AN AMAZING PERSON IN MY LIFE

I am in a joyous relationship with someone who truly loves me me

I AM WORTHY OF HAPPINESS AND LOVE

I AM READY FOR THE LOVE OF MY LIFE....

My heart is prepared to receive love

I ONLY ATTRACT HEALTHY RELATIONSHIPS.

THE UNIVERSE IS BRINGING MY SOULMATE TO ME

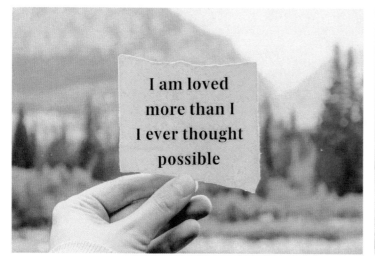

I am loved more than I I ever thought possible

MY PARTNER AND I ARE A TEAM

THIS IS MY
YEAR OF
DREAMS
COMING
TRUE

I AM
RESILIENT
AND CAN GET
THROUGH
ANYTHING

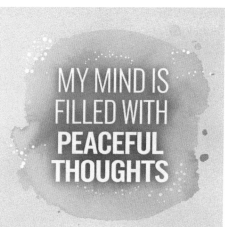

MY MIND IS
FILLED WITH
PEACEFUL
THOUGHTS

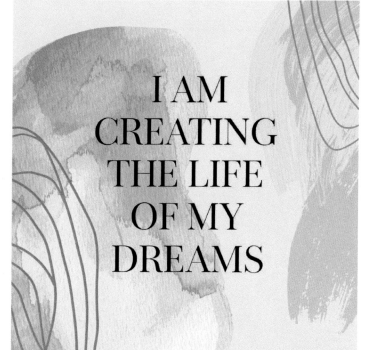

I AM
CREATING
THE LIFE
OF MY
DREAMS

I AM
AT
PEACE

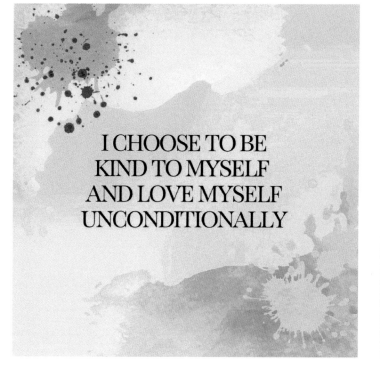

I CHOOSE TO BE
KIND TO MYSELF
AND LOVE MYSELF
UNCONDITIONALLY

I CHOOSE
COMPASSION
OVER
JUDGEMENT

I AM DESTINED TO TRAVEL

I AM GRATEFUL FOR THE MONEY I HAVE THAT ALLOWS ME TO TRAVEL

I AM LIVING MY BEST LIFE

I am grateful for for where I'm at. and excited about where I'm going

MY LIFE IS FULL OF ADVENTURE AND INCREDIBLE EXPERIENCES

I CAN MAKE TIME FOR TRAVEL THIS YEAR

I RELEASE CONTROL OF MY ITINERARY

I AM THANKFUL FOR SAFE JOURNEYS

I release my fears and can fully enjoy my journey

I'm going where I feel most alive

I AM MANIFESTING MIRACLES

I know a perfect house is coming my way

OUR NEW HOME IS *BEAUTIFUL*, BOUNTIFUL AND BLESSED

I have a beautiful home which is perfect for me.

I DESERVE MY DREAM HOME

I am Driving the car of My Dreams

I Love my Luxurious, Wealthy Lifestyle

I AM LIVING IN MY DREAM HOME

I CAN'T WAIT TO LIVE IN MY NEW HOME

I HAVE THE PERFECT HOME

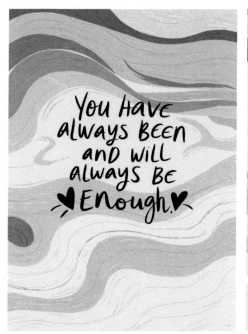

You have always been and will always be ♥ Enough. ♥

Your Heart Knows the Way

Prioritize your Peace

life is not a race. so embrace your own pace

you are worthy of every beautiful DREAM in your heart

YOU HAVE THE POWER TO CREATE YOUR OWN CLOSURE AND HEALING

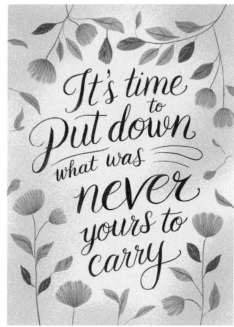

It's time to Put down what was never yours to carry

YOU DON'T NEED TO HAVE ALL THE ANSWERS

It's OK TO Say NO TO THINGS THAT DON'T Resonate

I GIVE MYSELF PERMISSION TO PURSUE MY DREAM JOB ✓

EMPLOYERS WILL NOTICE AND APPRECIATE MY SKILLS AND ABILITIES ✓

I AM SO IN DEMAND PEOPLE ARE LINING UP TO WORK WITH ME

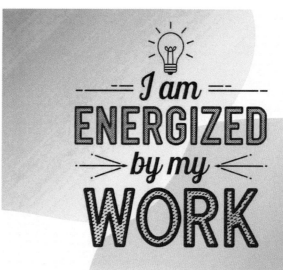

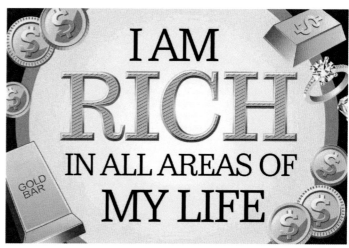

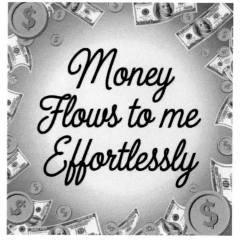

I AM EXACTLY WHO MY KID NEEDS

I am Leaving a Legacy of Love

I am a better parent when I take care of myself

I cherish the moments I spend with my family

Our Family bond is unbreakable and filled with LOVE

WHEN THERE IS CHAOS AROUND ME, I AM THE CALM

I WILL HAVE A BABY IN MY BELLY

I FOCUS ON THE JOY OF A FUTURE BABY

I AM A STRONG AND CAPABLE MOTHER

I WAS Made TO DO THIS

I FEEL SAFE AND COMFORTED BY MY FRIENDS

I CAN BE MYSELF WITH MY FRIENDS

my friendship circle is expanding

I am GRATEFUL for the FRIENDS I have

I attract wondeful people into my life

I AM WORTHY OF BEAUTIFUL FRIENDSHIPS

GOOD PEOPLE COME INTO MY LIFE EVERY DAY

True friendships find me easily

My friends bring joy and laughter into my life

i am blessed with incredible friends

I AM CAPABLE OF ACCOMPLISHING MY GOALS

TODAY I WILL DO SOMETHING MY FUTURE SELF WILL THANK ME FOR

I am making a difference in the world

I let go of what I can't control

I AM FREE OF NEGATIVITY AND SELF DOUBT

I CHOOSE TO LET GO OF FEAR

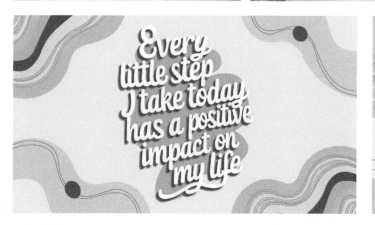

Every little step I take today has a positive impact on my life

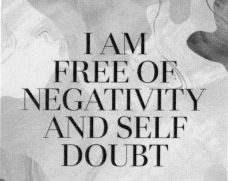

EVERY CHALLENGE I FACE IS AN OPPORTUNITY TO GROW

MY INNER SELF ALWAYS KNOWS WHAT TO DO

I TRUST MY GUT INSTINCTS

I BELIEVE THAT GOOD THINGS ARE COMING MY WAY

I CHOOSE TO
SPEAK UP
WHEN I HAVE HAD
ENOUGH

I FORGIVE MYSELF
FOR PAST MISTAKES
AND FAILURES

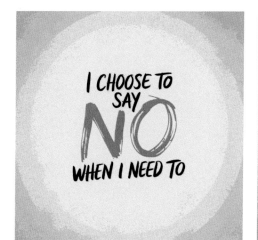

I CHOOSE TO
SAY
NO
WHEN I NEED TO

IF I
FALL,
I WILL GET
BACK UP
AGAIN

I AM
OPEN
TO NEW
ADVENTURES

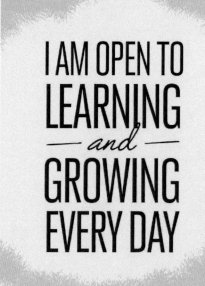

I AM OPEN TO
LEARNING
— and —
GROWING
EVERY DAY

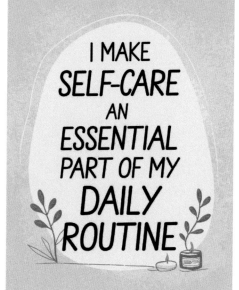

I MAKE
SELF-CARE
AN
ESSENTIAL
PART OF MY
DAILY
ROUTINE

My
Positive
Attitude
empowers me to
Overcome
Obstacles

I THINK
OUTSIDE THE BOX
TO SOLVE
PROBLEMS
EFFECTIVELY

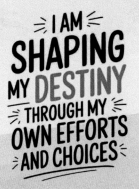

I AM
SHAPING
MY DESTINY
THROUGH MY
OWN EFFORTS
AND CHOICES

Hey there!

We just wanted to take a moment to say thank you for choosing our vision board book. We hope it's helping you manifest your dreams and inspiring you to be the best version of yourself.

If you're loving the book, we'd be over the moon if you could leave us a review on Amazon. We love reading your feedback, and we appreciate it more than you know.

Also, we have other books that we think you'll love too! Check out our collection of Vision Board titles at www.amazon.com/author/gloriagreene, or scan this QR code.

Looking for even more images?

Subscribe to our newsletter and we'll send you EVEN MORE downloadable images AND a FREE eBook that teaches you how to use the power of positive thinking and visualization to manifest your goals and desires. Scan the code below!

FREE E-BOOK

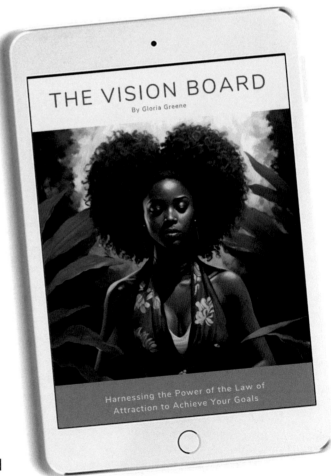

THE VISION BOARD
By Gloria Greene

Harnessing the Power of the Law of Attraction to Achieve Your Goals

Scan this QR code, or visit www.gloriagreene.com/Mdo9wY to download your FREE downloadable images AND eBook.

Made in the USA
Coppell, TX
27 December 2024

43570099R00026